Marketing for Emotions

By:

Rod Portelli

DEDICATION

**I dedicate this book to my kids as they grow &
become successful online for income.**

CONTENTS

ACKNOWLEDGMENTS

We all want to make money online. The key is Marketing to your intended audience, but How? Well reading Emotions in Marketing will help guide you in the right direction for you to market your product or service online.

1

Building customer'S
Relationships That Last

One of the ways a business builds its brand is to tug at the emotions of their audience. The way a customer and client work together and communicate can build long-lasting, meaningful relationships that turn clients into fans, and fans into clients. You can actually set out to build these relationships by using emotional marketing techniques.

1. Show Them That You Know Them

The more research you do into the needs and desires of your target audience, the more your audience will be able to tell that you're interested in them. When you show interest in them, it will make them interested in your business and you. When you discover something about your audience, let them know through your content and your actions.

2. Treat Them Right

So many times business owners have sales and special events to get new clients. What about the clients you already have? Keeping them is far more important than getting a new client, and less costly too. Do something special for your existing client base or fan base that shows them that you care about them. Give them a discount, or a special freebie, or something else that attaches them to you in a special way.

3. Be Transparent and Honest

One way to endear yourself to your audience is to always be transparent and honest. If you make a mistake, own up to it. If you change your views on something, it's okay to admit it. Doing so will endear you to your audience and make you appear so much more trustworthy to them.

4. Put People before Numbers

While you do things to help promote your business, it's important to keep your morals and remember that people are more important than numbers. If you put people first in your business, including yourself, you'll find that you naturally improve your bottom line. The more people trust you, the more they'll buy from you.

5. Be Fun When Appropriate

No one wants to feel as if they're communicating with a robot or someone who is not real. Be funny when it's appropriate so that you can show your humanity. Your humanness will shine through when you add some humor and fun to posts, emails, and even sales pages.

6. Be Responsive

Your customers expect to get an answer when they have a problem, and they expect it to be quickly. Provide many different ways for your audience to contact you. Explain to your audience at each method how long they can expect to wait for a response. Then follow up and do what you said you'd do.

7. Engage with Your Audience

Find ways to engage with your audience. Ask for their advice or ideas when it comes to a new product or service you're going to launch. They can help name it, help define what should be in it, and even how much you should charge for it. Your audience can also be your best source of word-of-mouth marketing.

Marketing for Emotions

8. Consider the Communication Format

Also, it's important to try to get an understanding of how people communicate within their environment. Communication online in chat, instant message, Twitter, or a blog, is far different from communicating on the telephone or in person. Even email is different from other methods of communication. It's imperative that you determine what is different and then make up for that with the type of communication they're using.

Building customer relationships that last is part of the goal of emotional marketing. When you've formed an attachment with the consumer, they will stick with you for years - through price increases, trials and tribulations, and more. You can't go wrong with building relationships.

2

Emotion In Marketing Communications

Great marketing seeks to tug at the emotional strings of the audience. Because if you can get them to think about things that trigger emotions - like happiness, longing, their sense of loss and more, you can also trigger them to answer your call to action. In fact, if you do it right, you can elicit those emotions in an audience just by them seeing your brand.

* Titles – Use emotional trigger words in your titles to get your audience's attention. Appeal to their sense of curiosity or loss. Words like "last chance" or "limited time offer" can and will go far in helping you get more click-through's and responses, too.

* Headlines – Whether it's an email marketing message or a blog post, it's important to develop creative headlines that don't confuse the reader but instead pique their attention. Use headlines such as "8 Ways to Ride a Bike" or "101 Ways to Avoid a Dating Disaster" to get their attention and make them want to read the article, eBook or content.

* Sub headers – Sometimes a sub header can help explain what's going to be inside so that you entice your audience to read the content, listen to the

Marketing for Emotions

podcast, or watch the video. You can think of them as taglines too. Just a few words to push your audience over the edge to consume the content will go far.

* Power Words and Phrases – Create a swipe file of power words and phrases that you can use when you want to trigger emotion in your audience. Words and phrases like "act now", "bonus", or "breakthrough" will work to get your audience into the mood you want them in to receive your messages.

* Transitions – Don't underestimate how important transition words are in text and speech. You can put your audience in exactly the mood you want them in with the right transition words. Words and phrases like "Listen…" or "Never again" or "Still not convinced" will go far in helping you explain a concept even more deeply.

* Calls to Action – Never, under any circumstances, forget to add in a call to action or two. Your CTA is important because without it your audience is unlikely to do what you want them to do based on the information you've provided. You have to tell them what to do. "Buy now", "Reserve your space", "Click here now to start your free trial", are all good CTAs, but you need to be as specific as possible.

* Closing Phrases – Another opportunity to tug at your audience's emotions is with closing phrases. You can use phrases like, "It's in your hands", "This is the final day that…" or "You're moments away from changing your life by …" and so forth. See how these words trigger certain emotions?

* Postscripts – Never forget the power of a P.S. when you're writing a letter, a sales page, or email. After you're done, just in case the audience is still reading instead of acting, include the P.S. and say something like, "P.S. Your satisfaction is always guaranteed" or "P.S. Act by Friday and you'll also get the free report" and so forth.

When you incorporate these trigger words and phrases into your marketing communications, you'll see an immediate return on investment. The power you have when it comes to using emotion in marketing is astronomical.

3

Emotional Marketing Online

Everything you do online can incorporate emotional marketing techniques. It doesn't matter if it's text, images, audio or visual in the form of video. First, let's talk a bit about the various types of emotions that you can elicit with your content.

Types of Emotion

* Visceral – When something impacts an audience member at the subconscious level, we say that the reaction is visceral. Your content, website design and so forth should evoke the feelings you want the visitor to feel without even thinking about it.

* Behavioral – Emotions and behavior go together hand in hand. When your audience member reads your content, listens to a video, or visits your website, the feelings they have should also elicit a behavioral response. For example, if a visitor comes to your website and feels frustrated with the navigation, their emotional feelings of frustration will elicit the response of leaving your website.

* Reflective – Once your audience member leaves your website, stops reading your eBook, or moves on past your content, it should stick with

Marketing for Emotions

them enough to cause a response of some sort based on their feelings. They might answer the CTA, or share your information with others, or think about it for a while, but they won't forget.

Aspects to Consider

Emotional marketing is a powerful tool that you can use in all your marketing efforts. It doesn't matter if it's a website, a sales page, a video or something else entirely - all aspects of it should be considered, such as:

* The Words – Know what words trigger emotion and action in your audience. Use words to focus on the benefits your product or service offers your audience. Remember that they want to know what's in it for them, not what's in it for you.

For example: Use trigger words like "Limited time offer..." or "Act now to completely change your life in the next 10 minutes..." You don't want to lie, but you do want to give it to them straight and tell them exactly what their benefits are for acting now.

* The Images – Images of people tend to bring forth more emotion for people. Let the face of the person demonstrate the emotion that you want the audience to feel as they look at your website, watch the video or consume other content that you offer.

For example: If you're writing about freedom and how your audience can experience freedom, try using a picture of something that demonstrates freedom to your audience. Use also a typical person that could be part of your audience, showing the emotional release they feel as they realize they have true freedom.

* The Colors – Some colors evoke different emotions based on culture, sex, and many other factors, so it's extra important to understand exactly who your audience is. You want the colors you choose to elicit the right emotions in your audience.

For example: If you want your audience to feel as if they should be excited and passionate about something, choose known passion colors like red and orange. If you want them to feel happy and free, choose a color like yellow to emulate the color of sunshine which makes people joyful. Do check to ensure that the culture you're marketing to does not have a different idea.

In order to accomplish that, you need to understand your audience completely so that you realize what their emotional needs are, plus what emotions trigger action for them. You can learn this by surveying your audience, getting to know them more, and asking for a lot of feedback as you create new products and services for them.

4

Emotions and Customer Loyalty Go Hand in Hand

Emotions affect every part of our lives. From our friendships to what we eat and what we buy, everything is affected by emotions - whether we realize them or not. If you want to be serious about marketing, you have to understand how to evoke emotions in your audience that encourages customer loyalty as well as purchasing. In fact, emotions are often more important than other factors when consumers make decisions.

* Understand What Your Brand Is – Your brand is a mental and emotional representation of your products and services. When a consumer thinks of your brand and you've done your job by branding your business, they will feel an emotional attachment and loyalty toward your version of the product or service. This is true even if there is competition that produces exactly what you do. Even if your price is more expensive, their loyalty and emotions keep them with you.

* Benefits over Features – One thing that elicits emotions in a person is learning about the benefits of a product or service. Consumers don't care about attributes, features or facts; they care more about what the product or service does for them.

* Experiences Matter – One thing that affects emotions exponentially, and by extension customer loyalty, is experience. If you can ensure that every customer has great a experience no matter where they are within the product funnel, then you can ensure good emotions that encourage loyalty which they'll share with others.

* Emotions and Reason – At first glance you may feel as if emotion and reason don't work together. But, the truth is that if you can combine emotional cues with reason, you'll affect your customers' loyalty at a much higher rate. Emotions require you to use triggers, but reason requires you not to exaggerate or lie.

* Emotions Build Trust – When you know exactly the words to use and the experiences to offer your audience, you will build trust that cannot be broken. People tend to look back on their experiences with a brand and judge future potential based on those experiences. Seek to provide awesome experiences and the trust you build will grow your business exponentially.

* Share Your Mission – Consumers love businesses that have a mission outside of the bottom line. For example, if you can connect your business to a charity that your audience would enjoy being part of, or you can demonstrate sound employment practices, offer excellent benefits and show care of other humans, you can cause your audience to become emotionally attached to you.

* Engagement Builds Community – Another way to encourage customer loyalty is to make your customer feel as if they're part of a community. The emotions they develop being part of a close-knit community will translate into them also being loyal to your brand. Engage with your customers by creating a Facebook group or message board and keep discussions going.

* Make Your Costumers Feel Special – Work to build special relationships with your customers individually and as a group. Find ways to make them feel special by offering consumer loyalty discounts, specials, freebies and other offers. Don't just make all the great offers for new customers.

Remember to treat your customers generously and look at them as human beings instead of wallets or ATMs. Customers can tell if they're not being treated well and will go elsewhere - no matter how good the value you offer is. That's because emotions and loyalty go hand in hand.

5

The Number One Emotion You Want to Trigger

If you can get this one thing right you can explode your business. It's the one emotional marketing trick that you want to exploit and get right - getting your audience to trust you. Trust is the one emotion that makes your audience want to give you money. Money is very personal and your audience must trust you to give you some of it. Here's how to earn that trust.

* Publish Relevant Content Regularly – Showing that you're dependable will go far in helping to develop trust with your audience. If you publish blog posts, email newsletters, or other material regularly, it will prove that you're in this for the long haul. And this helps push you to "authority" level and will cause people to trust you more.

* Tell Both Sides of the Story – When you are giving examples for anything, whether product or service, telling the pros and cons is always a good way to get people to trust you. If you are able to be truthful about the drawbacks of your own services or

products or those that you recommend, your audience will trust you as the real deal.

* Always Disclose Your Biases – If you are doing a review on a book, product, service or anything else, it's always important to tell the viewers the truth about any biases you may have. If you were given the item free to review, say so. If you were paid for your review, state it. Not only will this help people trust you better, it's also the law.

* Avoid Over-Pitching Products – When you always revert to sales language in all your content, people get tired of it. They expect a sales tone when looking at a sales page, but not when reading a blog. Be very careful not to confuse the two. Yes, you want a call to action, but you also want to avoid turning away viable audience members.

* Under Promise and Over Deliver – The danger of sales pages is the possibility of overstating what the product or service offers or the problems it solves. Instead, ensure that you can deliver even more than they expected once they purchase. Why? Because you want them to buy from you again and you want them to tell others about you. Word of mouth is the ultimate way to get the trust of others.

* Show Your Face – People trust those whom they can see. Online that can be more difficult, but if you post a picture of yourself and keep it updated, it will help them to trust you more. They'll see you as a real person instead of as a heartless business entity.

* Engage in Real Time – Beware of too much automation when it comes to social media. You want to engage with others in real time. This will further the trust that your audience is developing with you. They will feel important when you answer questions personally, and find ways to engage in real time.

* Make Videos – The next best thing to real life is a video. Videos help show what you know as if you're with the person

Marketing for Emotions

live. You can actually do an event live on Google Hangouts, then post the video later. This gives you the best of both worlds. Live engagement with the Google Hangout and recorded videos for others who missed it the first time around.

Developing trust is a process; it's a long-term marketing strategy that will pay off again and again. When you get just one person to trust you, they will tell ten others, and those ten others will each tell ten more people. The trust will spread far and wide until the very mention of your business name will mean trust. Ok, maybe it won't go that far, but you never know.

6

Trigger Words to Use in

emotional marketing

When you engage in emotional marketing, you'll want to learn the trigger words to use to garner specific emotions for your audience. Words change the significance, attitude and impulse of your audience to act. As they say, words are important. Words have meaning, and you'll want to use them very carefully as you form your marketing messages.

There are roughly ten emotions that you want to trigger in your marketing messages. You don't have to trigger them all in each message, but shoot for two or three and you'll have a winning marketing message. Let's go over the ten different emotions you can work on triggering in your audience, and how to go about it.

1. Community – People love the feeling of belonging to a tribe. We tend to flock together with those who are like us, and we like feeling included in a community. If you can make your audience feel as if they're part of something bigger than themselves by working with you or buying your products, you'll create a customer for life.

2. Competition – Everyone has a bit of a competitive streak; you can trigger your audience's competitive side by making them feel as if they might miss out. If you're only accepting five new customers for a particular offering, and you have a list of 500, it's more than likely you'll fill your roster within minutes of making the offer.

Marketing for Emotions

3. Fear – Making your audience believe and realize that if they don't act now they'll miss out on the offer, or that they can't live without your offer, will make your audience fearful that they'll be less if they don't have it.

4. Indulgence – Not only do consumers want to feel indulged, they also want to be spoiled right now. People love instant gratification and if they know that help is on the way right now, and it's free, they're going to trade their email address for your free offer straight away.

5. Guilt – In the realm of charities and not for profits, eliciting guilt is not hard to do. You can use guilt in your marketing efforts if you can come up with a slant. For example, if you are selling a work-from-home business idea, you could appeal to the guilt of mothers and fathers who must leave the home to work.

6. First Adoption – People like to be the ones who lead the way in choosing new products, technology, and services. Make the audience feel special and smart about their choice to buy your products or use your services.

7. Popularity – People want to be like their heroes and if you can offer them a way to do that, you have succeeded in making them feel like a trendsetter who is ahead of their peers and one step above others.

8. Time – Often times what you're really selling is time. If you are more explicit in the language you use regarding time (such as by using words like "now"), you can evoke feelings that make the audience feel as if the time to buy what you're offering is now.

9. Trust – Using words (and meaning them) like "guaranteed", "full refund" and so forth will help your audience trust you more. When it comes to marketing, trust is possibly the most powerful way to get more business. People don't want to open their wallet if they don't trust you. Prove them right when they buy from you.

10. Value - If you can prove your value and that you'll save them time, or money, or something else, your audience will want to give you a try. This is your chance to under promise and over deliver.

Using trigger words to elicit the emotions you want your audience to feel will go far in helping you develop your marketing messages.

7

Understand Why People Spend Money

When it comes to creating marketing messages, especially those that trigger emotions, it helps to understand the reasons why people spend money in the first place. If you can understand why your audience opens their wallet to buy, you can trigger them to do so whenever you want them to.

* To Portray an Image – People want others to perceive them in a certain way. That need often drives them to buy things to help them keep that image, not only for others to see them that way but also to see themselves that way.

* To Avoid a Bad Feeling – Whether it's the idea they'll miss out on something awesome, or some other bad feeling, avoiding a bad feeling is a powerful motivator to buy something. If you can show how your product or service helps your audiences avoid a bad feeling, they'll be more likely to buy.

* To Gain or Earn Freedom – A good example is a housekeeper or

Marketing for Emotions

virtual assistant. Is a housekeeper selling a clean home, or more time? Is a virtual assistant selling document processing or more time? If you can be clear about what it is you're really selling, you can and will entice your audience to buy from you more often.

* To Fit In With the Community – Everyone likes being part of the "in" crowd and part of a community. If making a specific purchase will make them more of a part of the community, they will make it happen.

* Immediate Gratification – People like getting what they want, when they want it. If you can offer them an instantaneous way to give them what they want, they will most certainly take the bait. The important thing is to deliver on your promises.

* To Gain a Sense of Power – When people buy something they view as potentially life changing, they feel powerful and in charge of their lives. If you can offer something super special that solves a very specific problem and evokes feelings of power in your audience, you'll have a winner on your hands.

* To Prove or Gain Self-Worth – Some people, maybe people in your audience, lack self-worth and need a way to get it. If you can offer them that feeling when they buy your products or use your services, you'll sell a lot.

* To Solve a Problem – One of the most obvious reasons people spend money is to solve a problem. Show them how your product or service solves their problems, and they'll buy from you when the price is right.

It's important to study your audience so that you know how to trigger these feelings within them, and know which ones they use when they choose to buy. If you can find the trigger that keeps your audience from saying no, you'll explode your business beyond your wildest dreams.

8

What Is Emotional Marketing?

Emotional marketing is a term thrown around in the marketing world that means basically what you think. It means that you use various words, colors and images to evoke certain emotions in the audience in all your marketing messages. There is an entire science involved in marketing that studies the effect of the colors, images and words on the page and how they affect the consumer.

There are eight emotions that can be brought out by various words:

1. Sadness
2. Fear
3. Anger
4. Surprise
5. Disgust
6. Anticipation
7. Joy
8. Trust

Each emotion has various stages and strengths that we tend to call other emotions. For example, joy, anger and anticipation can translate into

Marketing for Emotions

passion. Feelings of anticipation and joy can be called optimism. The trick is that each audience has their own trigger words that will evoke certain emotions, and they have certain emotions that will trigger various actions for that particular audience.

Encourage Sharing

For the most part, emotions like joy and trust make us want to share with others. That being the case, you may want to make your audience feel trusting and happy to get them to share their information with you and to share you with their friends. Each audience has its own language that elicits trust and happiness. It's important to learn it.

Make Them Want to Help

If you want people to empathize then you should seek to evoke feelings of sadness and loss in the audience members. Think of the ASPCA commercials where they show abused and starving animals during a sad song. This makes the audience feel sad and terrible and want to help. Since they're a well-known organization with a good reputation, trust is already there. Each time the commercials air, many people donate.

Go Viral

If you want a post to go viral, you should pair it with some anger, disgust and anticipation or fear. Be sure to give your audience members a way out of these bad feelings, which is to buy what you're offering. This works because these feelings are extraordinarily powerful and have lasting consequences.

Feelings First

When engaging in emotional marketing, it's important to realize that feelings go first. People feel, and then they buy. If you want more people to buy, make them feel something that leads them to buying what you're offering.

Examples of Emotional Marketing

A great lesson in the way emotional marketing works is to watch the entire series of Mad Men, especially the early episodes. You can learn so much about how the copywriters and ad men dealt with their audience's emotions through the written word, images, and eventually TV commercials.

In the meantime, here are some examples to take a look at:

* Procter & Gamble – This award-winning ad elicits feelings of community, belonging, family and pride very well.

Link - https://youtu.be/8ywO8DR-5NY

* Netflix Commercial – This commercial makes you want to belong to the community of watchers and see the shows that only are on Netflix, due to the innovative, funny, and interesting shows.

Link - https://youtu.be/0SZv2vPdj6g

* Pfizer – This commercial pulls at the heartstrings to promote the message of a drug company.

Link - https://youtu.be/OAlyHUWjNjE

What commercials can you find that evokes emotions in you? What about sales pages, or blog posts, or other types of advertising?

9

Why Emotions Matter in Marketing

The truth is, nothing can elicit a response quite like the right emotion. The thing marketers want most from their audience is a response. They want them to answer their calls to action. They want them to take action, engage, buy, join or do something. And, the best way to do that is to evoke the right emotions that cause the right action to take place.

* More Likely to Go Viral – Any marketing message that evokes a strong emotional response is more likely to "go viral" than a bland message that doesn't pull at any emotional strings. The emotion most likely to be shared widely, however, is anger, so you need to tread lightly when it comes to that. Give your audience a way out of their anger by taking an action.

* More Engaging – When you get your audience to feel something strongly, the advertisement automatically becomes more engaging. Content that evokes an emotion, then solves a

problem, is gold when it comes to emotional marketing.

* More Useful – Most emotional content is going to prove to be more useful than content that isn't as heartfelt. Highlight the social implications of the product and service and you'll create a fan for life.

* More Motivating – Elicit emotions like confidence or fear in your audience, and you're going to motivate them to answer your CTA faster and easier than if you don't use those emotional triggers.

* More Compelling – Bringing emotions to your marketing messages will make every message more compelling to your audience. They're going to be more likely to hear your entire message or read your entire message, thus getting more of the information they need to make a buying decision.

* Better Branding – If you want your brand to represent a specific emotion, you can do that. Think about the brands you know and what emotions they elicit. Coke brings people together, Amazon makes all things possible with extreme personalization, FedEx makes promise and keeps them, and so forth. What does your brand represent?

* Science Says So – Many neuroscientists and psychologists are involved in marketing companies these days, and are doing a lot of study into the power of emotional marketing. They say it works and science has the proof.

* Demonstrates Passion – People want to be part of something special and if you can show in your marketing messages the passion you have for your niche and for your customers, you can achieve more than you ever thought possible.

Using emotions helps all of us make choices in life; your audience is no different. Evoke the right emotions, and you can get your audience to do almost anything you want. Provide a quality product or service that solves serious issues and problems for your audience, and you'll cultivate a life-long customer due to the trust you'll develop.

10

Why Engage in Emotional Marketing

Emotional marketing has always been around, but lately it's caught on with many mainstream brands. Even companies that on the surface aren't really emotional by nature have found ways to include emotional triggers into advertising. It's that old line that "sex" sells. However, the truth is that it's not just sex - it's emotion that sells. Sex just triggers a specific emotion, such as the need to belong, that causes people to want to buy.

The most effective emotions that you can trigger in your audience with the right words, images and colors are:

* Affection
* Amusement
* Delight
* Excitement
* Happiness
* Hope
* Interest
* Joy

Marketing for Emotions

* Pleasure
* Surprise

These emotions usually elicit positivity in your audience. It's true that other emotions may get more response, such as anger, but you have to be very careful with anger so that you don't have a situation that backfires on you.

The more dangerous emotions that you can also trigger with the right words, images and colors are:

* Anger
* Contempt
* Despair
* Doubt
* Embarrassment
* Frustration
* Guilt
* Hurt
* Politeness
* Shame

With the right type of emotional marketing you can:

* Turn Wants to Needs: Everyone wants to be rich, work on the beach, or have their perfect kitchen, but they aren't really "needs" - they are wants. Many people will not spend money on wants over needs. With the right emotional triggers you can turn a want into a need that someone needs so badly that they'll buy it right now, no matter the price.

* Prove Value: It might seem weird to say but if you can trigger the right emotions, you can also prove the value of your products and services. The way to do that is to sell what the product or service provides. Is it free time? What intangible concept does your product give the buyer? Exploit that.

* Provoke a Sense of Belonging: If you really want to get people to want to follow you anywhere, make them feel like a special part of your community, such as a VIP or a member of your "inner circle" or "mastermind" group.

* Create a Viral Trend: Emotional things are more likely to be shared by your audience on social media and become viral. If you can identify the

ideas that will go viral, as well as the emotions that trigger more sharing, you can create a trend of your own.

* Connect with Customers: The right words will make your audience feel very connected with and close to you. They'll become your biggest fans and turn word of mouth into an avalanche of potential leads for you.

Emotional marketing can change your marketing efforts completely and make your sales pages, blog posts, and other marketing content really stand out. Study your audience and determine not only what they need in terms of products and services, but also what they need to hear in terms of trigger words - words that evoke emotions that make them do something you want them to do. This could be something like joining your mailing list, or buying your products, or using your services.

ABOUT THE AUTHOR

ROD G.-PORTELLI JR. is the author of *God's Revelation.*
Publishing Many Books and *How To Use Your Words to*
Steer Your life in the direction you need. He lives in Nv with
his family. Rod loves educating and inspiring People and the
world to succeed and live the life God Almighty has for them.

Jer. 29:11 (NIV) **¹¹ For I know the plans I have for
you," declares the LORD, "plans to prosper you
and not to harm you, plans to give you hope
and a future.**

The adventure continues . . .

Follow the adventures of Rod here at:
youtube.com/thegenesislife

Stay In touch with the author via:

Email: thegenesislife@gmail.com

Thank you very much for your time in reading my book. I would
appreciate if you would kindly post a positive review on amozon.

www.ingramcontent.com/pod-product-compliance
Lightning Source LLC
Chambersburg PA
CBHW071832200526
45169CB00018B/1417